What Else Can I Pla

Alto Saxophone
Grade One

Series Editor: Mark Mumford

Music arranged and processed by
Barnes Music Engraving Ltd
East Sussex TN22 4HA, England

Published 1996

© International Music Publications Limited
Southend Road, Woodford Green, Essex IG8 8HN, England

Reproducing this music in any form is illegal and forbidden
by the Copyright, Designs and Patents Act 1988

Introduction

In this *What Else Can I Play?* collection you'll find sixteen popular tunes that are both challenging and entertaining.

The pieces have been carefully selected and arranged to create ideal supplementary material for young saxophonists who are either working towards or have recently taken a Grade One saxophone examination.

As the student progresses through the volume, technical demands increase and new concepts are introduced which reflect the requirements of the major Examination Boards. Suggestions and guidelines on breathing, dynamics and tempo are given for each piece, together with technical tips and performance notes.

Pupils will experience a wide variety of music, ranging from folk and classical through to showtunes and popular songs, leading to a greater awareness of musical styles.

Whether it's for light relief from examination preparation, or to reinforce the understanding of new concepts, this collection will enthuse and encourage all young saxophone players.

Note: references to fingering within this book use Thumb 1 2 3 4.

All through the night

Welsh Traditional

© 1996 International Music Publications Limited, Woodford Green, Essex IG8 8HN

Puff the magic dragon

Words and Music by Peter Yarrow and Leonard Lipton

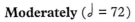

© 1963 & 1996 Pepamar Music Corp, Honalee Melodies and Cherry Lane Publishing, USA
Warner/Chappell Music Ltd, London W1Y 3FA and Cherry Lane Music Ltd, London WC2H 0EA

I'm looking over a four leaf clover

Words by Mort Dixon, Music by Harry Woods

© 1927 & 1996 Remick Music Corp, USA
Francis Day & Hunter Ltd, London WC2H 0EA and Redwood Music Ltd, London NW1 8BD

Men of Harlech

Traditional

© 1996 International Music Publications Limited, Woodford Green, Essex IG8 8HN

The Quartermaster store

Traditional

© 1996 International Music Publications Limited, Woodford Green, Essex IG8 8HN

Fantasie-impromptu

Frédéric Chopin

© 1996 International Music Publications Limited, Woodford Green, Essex IG8 8HN

Land of my fathers

Traditional

© 1996 International Music Publications Limited, Woodford Green, Essex IG8 8HN

Edelweiss

Words by Oscar Hammerstein II, Music by Richard Rodgers

© 1959 Richard Rodgers and Oscar Hammerstein II

Copyright renewed. This arrangement © 1996 Williamson Music

Williamson Music owner of publication and allied rights throughout the world

Les bicyclettes de Belsize

Les Reed and Barry Mason

© 1968 & 1996 Donna Music Ltd, London WC2H 0EA

What Else Can I Play?
Alto Saxophone
Grade One

All through the night

Welsh Traditional

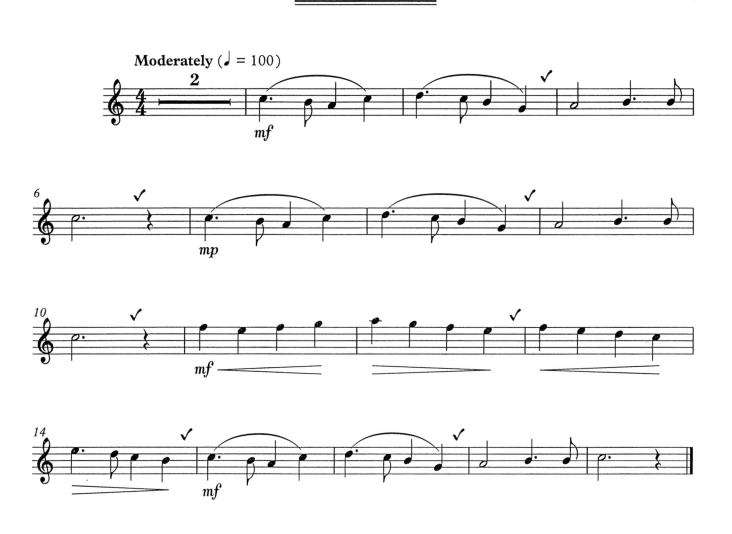

'All Through The Night' is the English name by which the Welsh folk-song 'Ar Hyd y Nos' is known. This song is a soothing lullaby, not to be confused with the romantic duet of the same title, written by American songwriter Cole Porter for his show *Anything Goes*.

Play *legato* and keep the crotchets even. From bar 11 use the dynamics to bring out the expression, but keep your embouchure firm as you play the higher notes. Don't play too close to the tip of the mouthpiece or the notes will sound thin.

FABER PRINT
AUTHORISED COPY
WHEN RED

© 1996 International Music Publications Limited, Woodford Green, Essex IG8 8HN

2

Puff the magic dragon

Words and Music by Peter Yarrow and Leonard Lipton

For years this was one of the most frequently requested songs on children's radio. That is until someone suggested that the words are about smoking! In fact the song describes a land of enchantment, called Honah Lee, and tells of how, in growing up, we risk losing touch with childhood fantasies.

Keep the crotchets even all the way through this tune; resist shortening notes when you come to a breath mark! Take care on repeated notes, each one needs to be clearly tongued. Keep your phrasing smooth and sustained.

© 1963 & 1996 Pepamar Music Corp, Honalee Melodies and Cherry Lane Publishing, USA
Warner/Chappell Music Ltd, London W1Y 3FA and Cherry Lane Music Ltd, London WC2H 0EA

I'm looking over a four leaf clover

Words by Mort Dixon, Music by Harry Woods

Harry Woods and Mort Dixon were American writers who created numerous popular songs in the 1920s and 30s. This particular ballad was a great success for the all-round entertainer Al Jolson. The song enjoyed a revival after the release of the film *Jolson Sings Again* (1949) which told the story of Jolson's wartime service tours.

Keep the tune light and the crotchets slightly detached. Observe the breath marks carefully as they give you a guide to the phrasing. Take deep breaths where marked and use pressure from your diaphragm to support the sound – this will help you sustain the long notes without losing volume.

© 1927 & 1996 Remick Music Corp, USA
Francis Day & Hunter Ltd, London WC2H 0EA and Redwood Music Ltd, London NW1 8BD

Men of Harlech

Traditional

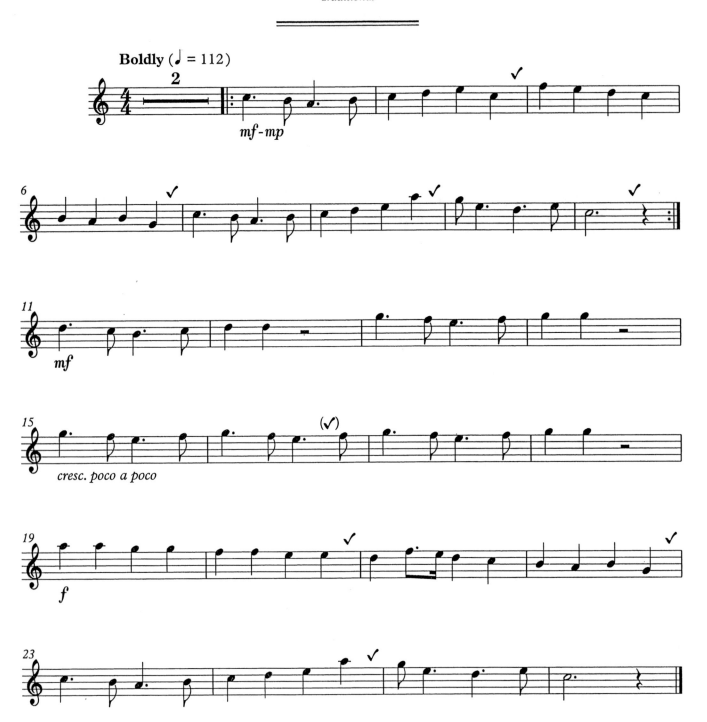

This stirring traditional song tells of battle between the Celts and their Saxon foe. Harlech is a town in north-west Wales, whose name means 'above the boulders'. To this day the ruins of an impressive castle stand there, on rocks overlooking the sea-shore.

A good strong rhythm runs through this tune. Keep strictly in time, making sure you don't cut notes short when you come to a breath mark. After the build up to the climax, in bars 15 to 18, let the notes sing out with a glorious full tone. The dynamic marks at the beginning mean that you play *mf* first time through and *mp* for the repeat.

© 1996 International Music Publications Limited, Woodford Green, Essex IG8 8HN

The Quartermaster store

Traditional

Moderately (♩ = 100)

The Quartermaster store is where rations would be held for the troops. This jokey song tells just what the soldiers think of the food they're getting!

Each of the phrases starts at the end of the bar: the breath marks will help you identify them. Try to keep the dotted rhythms 'spitting' in the first eight bars (remember that terrible food). Don't let the dotted rhythm become lazy. From bar 8 onwards, the song's chorus is a mock hymn, so make a contrast by playing the crotchets smoothly.

© 1996 International Music Publications Limited, Woodford Green, Essex IG8 8HN

Fantasie-impromptu

Frédéric Chopin

Polish-born composer and pianist Frédéric Chopin (1810–1849) lived much of his life in Paris, where he entertained fashionable society with performances of his lyrical, flowing music. The title 'Impromptu' was often used in the nineteenth century to describe a short piano piece. This tune was later taken to create the American show song 'I'm Always Chasing Rainbows'.

The word *cantabile* means to play in a singing style. See if you can achieve this effect throughout. Play quietly and smoothly, tonguing lightly and holding notes to their full value. Look ahead for the marked B flats, keeping the key firmly under control when returning to the A.

© 1996 International Music Publications Limited, Woodford Green, Essex IG8 8HN

Land of my fathers

Traditional

Majestically (♩ = 88)

This is the Welsh national anthem, a moving song which declares a patriotic love for Wales. Its original title is *Mae Hen Wlad Fy Nhadau*.

The tune should be fairly slow and majestic. Follow the phrasing carefully; each one begins on the last beat of the bar. The quavers must be controlled, so don't let your fingers run away with you. There are a few F sharps to play – be prepared!

© 1996 International Music Publications Limited, Woodford Green, Essex IG8 8HN

Edelweiss

Words by Oscar Hammerstein II, Music by Richard Rodgers

The edelweiss is the national flower of Switzerland. This song is sung by Maria in the celebrated musical *The Sound Of Music*. Writers Rodgers and Hammerstein were responsible for some of the most famous musicals ever staged, including *South Pacific*, *The King And I*, *Carousel* and *Oklahoma!*

This beautiful melody requires sensitive playing. Observe the dynamic marking *piano* and play right through to the end of each bar to keep the phrases flowing. Don't forget the B flats, which are indicated in the key signature.

© 1959 Richard Rodgers and Oscar Hammerstein II

Copyright renewed. This arrangement © 1996 Williamson Music

Williamson Music owner of publication and allied rights throughout the world

Les bicyclettes de Belsize

Les Reed and Barry Mason

This song was a hit in 1968 for singer Englebert Humperdinck. He had previously performed under the less eccentric title of Gerry Dorsey but found greater success when relaunched with a name borrowed from the opera composer. The team that wrote this song also supplied Englebert's number one hit 'The Last Waltz' and provided Tom Jones with the dramatic 'Delilah'.

This piece is a waltz, with three beats in the bar and a slight emphasis on the first beat. Watch out for B flats, the key is F major. It might help to practise the scale of F major as most of the tune's phrases are related to it. Count the last two bars carefully.

© 1968 & 1996 Donna Music Ltd, London WC2H 0EA

I'm Popeye the sailor man

Words and Music by Sammy Lerner

This is the theme tune for the popular cartoon which first appeared in 1931 and finally ceased production in 1967, 454 adventures later. The exploits of Popeye and his friend Olive Oyl always promoted the idea that spinach is good for you!

Each phrase starts on an upbeat. If you place a slight emphasis at the beginning of the bar this will help shape the phrases and achieve something of Popeye's cheerful swagger! When the tune leaps down to the lower notes, relax your embouchure a little and remember not to bite onto the reed.

© 1934 & 1996 Famous Music Corp, USA
Used by permission of Music Sales Ltd, London W1Y 3FA

John Peel

John Woodcock Graves

'D'ye ken John Peel ...' ('Do you know John Peel?') asks the song, attributed to the writer John Woodcock Graves and thought to date from around 1820. The tune is older still and was traditionally known as 'Bonnie Annie'. The gentleman in question was a hunting man, probably from Cumberland.

There are quite a few repeated notes which will require clear tonguing and careful finger work. Keep the notes short and under control, taking quick breaths where marked. Listen carefully to the intonation of the octave intervals in bars 7 and 15.

© 1996 International Music Publications Limited, Woodford Green, Essex IG8 8HN

Bye bye blackbird

Words by Mort Dixon, Music by Ray Henderson

This cheerful song dates from 1926 and, like many other songs from the twenties and thirties, demonstrates how a simple catchy melody can be immensely successful. The piece has been interpreted by literally hundreds of artists and has been used in at least four films.

Lots of contrast is needed in this piece. The first section requires light staccato tonguing which then changes to smoother, legato playing in the middle section. Look out for the G sharps in bars 22 and 30. Remember to press the G sharp key firmly, keeping the third and fourth fingers moving together.

© 1926 & 1996 Remick Music Corp, USA

Francis Day & Hunter Ltd, London WC2H 0EA and Redwood Music Ltd, London NW1 8BD

Frosty the snowman

Words and Music by Steve Nelson and Jack Rollins

Written in 1950, this light-hearted song about a snowman who came to life is now one of radio and television's perennial Christmas melodies.

The tune can really bounce along; keep a brisk tempo and for the staccato notes, have your tongue near the tip of the reed. Play more smoothly in the quieter middle section (bars 18 to 26), in contrast to the spirited opening tune which returns at bar 27.

© 1950 & 1996 Intersong USA Inc, USA
Carlin Music Corp, London NW1 8BD

Rudolph the red-nosed reindeer

Words and Music by Johnny Marks

This song is a Christmas favourite. Poor Rudolph is picked on by the other reindeer because of his bright red nose. However, when Santa Claus asks Rudolph to guide his sleigh through a foggy Christmas Eve, he soon becomes the most popular reindeer of all. Can you name the other reindeer?

Make your playing light and bouncy and aim for a contrast between staccato and legato phrasing. For the high notes be sure your embouchure is firm, especially when leaping across wide intervals. Don't panic over the syncopated rhythm; as long as you remember that the first and third beats are strong, you shouldn't go wrong!

© 1949 & 1996 St Nicholas Music Inc, USA
Warner/Chappell Music Ltd, London W1Y 3FA

I'm forever blowing bubbles

Words and Music by Jaan Kenbrovin and John Kellette

This popular music-hall piece appears in many different arrangements but is a special favourite with close harmony singers and the supporters of a certain football team!

Let the tune float along smoothly, lightly stressing the first beat of each phrase. Keep your fingers firmly under control, taking particular care over the change from F sharp to F natural. Bars 19 and 20 might need extra practice; the right hand third and fourth fingers must move together or a D might creep in!

© 1919 & 1996 Remick Music Corp, USA

B Feldman & Co Ltd, London WC2H 0EA and Redwood Music Ltd, London NW1 8BD

O sole mio

Traditional

This Italian aria dates from 1899 and is a popular showpiece for operatic tenors. The tune has been hijacked on more than one occasion; Aaron Schroeder and Wally Gold created 'It's Now Or Never', which was a Number One hit in the UK for Elvis Presley, in 1960. Later still, a memorable version of the operatic original was used for an ice-cream commercial on television.

You can use *tempo rubato* in this piece, meaning that instead of keeping strictly in time you hold back a little or move forward on the phrases, for expressive effect. Make sure your pianist knows what you are doing though! E flats, of course, have the same fingering as D sharp. At bars 11 and 27, try to ensure all four right-hand fingers move precisely together, playing G to E flat. This may be tricky!

© 1996 International Music Publications Limited, Woodford Green, Essex IG8 8HN

Reproduced and printed by Halstan & Co. Ltd., Amersham, Bucks., England

I'm Popeye the sailor man

Words and Music by Sammy Lerner

© 1934 & 1996 Famous Music Corp, USA
Used by permission of Music Sales Ltd, London W1Y 3FA

John Peel

John Woodcock Graves

© 1996 International Music Publications Limited, Woodford Green, Essex IG8 8HN

Bye bye blackbird

Words by Mort Dixon, Music by Ray Henderson

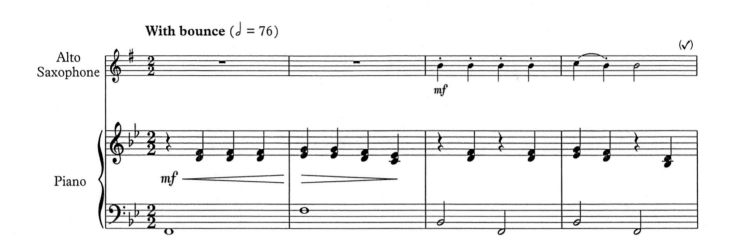

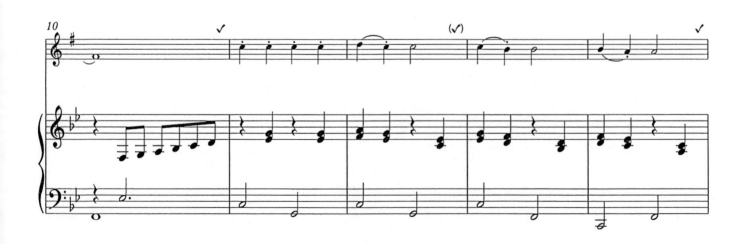

© 1926 & 1996 Remick Music Corp, USA
Francis Day & Hunter Ltd, London WC2H 0EA and Redwood Music Ltd, London NW1 8BD

Frosty the snowman

Words and Music by Steve Nelson and Jack Rollins

© 1950 & 1996 Intersong USA Inc, USA
Carlin Music Corp, London NW1 8BD

Rudolph the red-nosed reindeer

Words and Music by Johnny Marks

© 1949 & 1996 St Nicholas Music Inc, USA
Warner/Chappell Music Ltd, London W1Y 3FA

I'm forever blowing bubbles

Words and Music by Jaan Kenbrovin and John Kellette

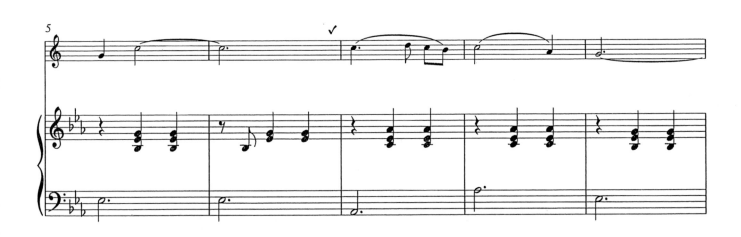

© 1919 & 1996 Remick Music Corp, USA

B Feldman & Co Ltd, London WC2H 0EA and Redwood Music Ltd, London NW1 8BD

O sole mio

Traditional

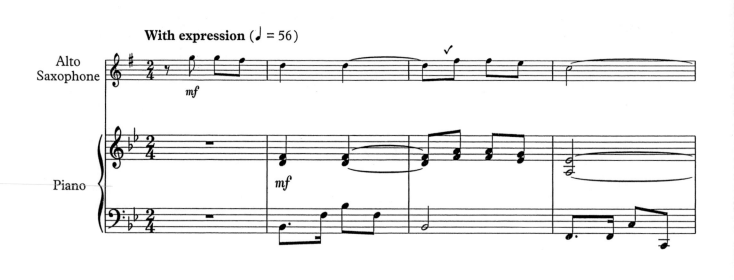

© 1996 International Music Publications Limited, Woodford Green, Essex IG8 8HN

Reproduced and printed by
Halstan & Co. Ltd., Amersham, Bucks., England

2/03